One
Woman's Choice

Rob Waring, *Series Editor*

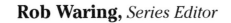

NATIONAL
GEOGRAPHIC
LEARNING

Australia · Brazil · Mexico · Singapore · United Kingdom · United States

Words to Know

This story is set in Africa, in the country of Tanzania [tænzəniə]. It happens on the south Maasai Steppe in the village of Kijungu [kidʒuŋgu], and in the city of Arusha [əruʃə].

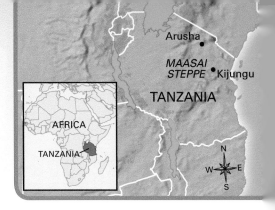

A **In an African Village.** Read the paragraph. Then match each word with the correct definition.

This story is about a woman, Flora Salonik [flɔrə sælənik], who lives in the tiny village of Kijungu on the Maasai Steppe in Tanzania. Flora's family grows a few crops and raises cattle for food. It's a very hard life without any modern conveniences like mail or telephones. They depend completely on the land for their livelihood.

1. steppe _____	**a.** large farm animals kept for their milk or meat
2. crops _____	**b.** a large area of land with grass and few or no trees
3. cattle _____	**c.** useful things that help make life more comfortable
4. conveniences _____	**d.** grain, vegetables, and fruit grown in large amounts
5. livelihood _____	**e.** way of earning money to live

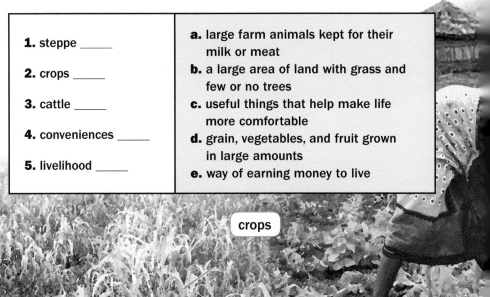

crops

B **Village or City?** Read the paragraph. Then complete the definitions with the correct form of the underlined words.

Flora lives in a village now, but she grew up in a big city. Sometimes she misses her lifestyle there. Having things like mail service and hospitals made life easier, and having good transport, such as buses and trains, made it simpler to get places. The village of Kijungu is very remote, so it's hard for Flora to keep in contact with her mother and sisters in the city. Sometimes she feels restless, and must now make an important choice: should she stay in the village with her family or return to the life she once knew?

1. The British term for cars, trains, buses, etc. is _____.

2. Something that is far away from everything is _____.

3. A _____ is a person or group's way of living.

4. _____ means that you are unable to stay still or to be quiet and calm because you are worried or bored.

cattle

A Small Village in Tanzania

Flora Salonik grew up in one of Tanzania's busiest cities, Arusha. She has a university education and speaks four languages. These days, however, she doesn't live the life one might expect an educated woman to live. She resides in a village, works on the land, and depends on the earth for her livelihood. She and her family have a small farm where they keep cattle and eat the food they grow. Flora's life has certainly changed since her younger years in Arusha. And it all happened because she fell in love with a man from the Dorobo people.

🎧 CD 2, Track 05

Flora talks about how the relationship started: "About ten years ago, I met this man. We fell in love and got married. We met in Tana, got talking, and started dating." After the two decided to get married, the change in lifestyle was significant for Flora. As soon as they were married, her husband, **Loshero**,[1] brought her to the tiny village of Kijungu on Tanzania's south Maasai Steppe. Here, they moved into a small **hut**[2] to live.

The remote village is a four-day journey on foot from Arusha. In fact, it's one of the most remote places in Tanzania. When her family said goodbye to Flora back in Arusha, they knew that she was leaving the comforts of the city and moving to a world without electricity or almost any modern conveniences. In this faraway village, it takes a forty-minute walk just to get water!

---

[1]**Loshero:** [ləʃɪərou]
[2]**hut:** a small, simple building often made of wood

Unlike some Dorobo people, Flora and Loshero raise cattle and grow crops to feed their family. Every day, Flora must get milk from the cows and gather plants for food. The Dorobo are one of the few **hunter-gatherer**[3] societies left in East Africa, and they usually live only on plants and animals from the wild. The Dorobo lifestyle means that Loshero often spends long periods away from home while hunting. While he does this, Flora is often left to care for their three children, their farm, and their home by herself. She gave up everything for Loshero, and now she hardly sees him.

Flora sometimes dreams of returning to the city, and occasionally even packs her possessions for the journey. "Sometimes I pack my stuff … ready to go back to Arusha," she says, "But I have children, so I can't go home." However, it doesn't stop her from dreaming. She dreams about returning to the city where she once lived and where her family is.

───────────────────

[3]**hunter-gatherer:** people who live on plants and animals from the wild

Many years have gone by since Flora left the city and moved to the village of Kijungu. In all that time she has had no contact with her family. In Kijungu, there is no mail service and there are no telephones—that means no phone calls or letters. Flora hasn't been able to communicate with her family since she came.

It's difficult for Flora to stop thinking about the past and she often looks at photographs of herself before she met Loshero. Sometimes she thinks about the way her life could have been. She also thinks about what she would have done in the city. But what can she do now? She can either take her children back to live in the city and leave Loshero in the village, or she can forget about her old life. Her husband doesn't know anything about the difficult choice that his wife must make, and she knows that she can't have both options.

Flora feels restless, and decides that the best action to take is to visit her hometown of Arusha. She feels that it may help her to make her difficult decision. As she begins the four-day walk early the next morning, she doesn't dare to look back at her children. It may be too painful for her. She's sad to leave them, but her neighbors will take care of them while she **figures out**[4] their future.

---

[4]**figure out:** find a solution to a question or problem

After her long walk, Flora finally arrives in the busy city of Arusha, which is the center of Tanzania's tourist and **safari**[5] businesses. Flora was born here and this is where she attended school, had her first job, and met her first boyfriend. Since she has been away for so long, the busy streets of her hometown are unfamiliar to Flora; they're so different from Kijungu.

As she walks down the street towards her childhood home, Flora isn't certain if her mother still lives in the same house. She doesn't even know if she's still alive. Flora finally arrives at the house where she once lived and where she last saw her mother. A few of the neighbors stop and stare at her, but Flora only has one thing on her mind: will her mother still be there?

---

[5]**safari:** an organized trip to look at or hunt wild animals, especially in Africa

Scan for Information

Scan page 15 to answer the questions:

1. Who's the first family member that Flora sees?

2. How does the person react to her return?

3. How long has it been since she has seen the person?

As Flora approaches her childhood home, a short, older woman rushes out to meet her. Flora's mother is still there! It's an emotional **reunion**[6] between mother and daughter. They hold each other, laugh, and cry.

Later, in her mother's house, the two women sit and talk. It's been a very long time, and they have much to discuss. Flora's mother explains: "It's [been] about 11 years since we saw each other. We didn't fight, we didn't have any **rows**,[7] she just left home. I am very happy to see her again. I don't want her to go back too soon. But if there is no choice, she will have to go because she has children, and her husband is waiting for her there." Flora's mother knows that Flora may decide to go back to Kijungu, but for now she's just happy to see her daughter.

---

[6] **reunion:** a time when people who have something in common come together again after a period apart
[7] **row:** (*British English*) a fight or disagreement

Flora stays with her mother in Arusha for a while. She then visits all the places she used to know, trying to relate to the person she used to be. She sits in the school that she went to as a girl, thinking about her past—and about her future. She considers her options for a long time, and it isn't an easy decision. Should she bring her children to Arusha, or return to her life in Kijungu? Whatever Flora decides, she knows that she will lose something important: her husband and family, or her past.

Finally, Flora makes her decision about her future and the future of her family: she chooses to go back to Kijungu. Later, back in the village, she talks about her decision: "I really want to come back to Kijungu. I feel [that I am] a Dorobo." She then continues, "My sisters didn't understand how I could live here. There's no transport, no hospitals; but I am happy here because of the land. I want to live here because this is my life." She then adds, "People say it is a hard place to live, but my home is here."

It's obvious from Flora's description of her feelings that it was a difficult decision for her. Choosing between a new family and the old is never easy; but this woman has made her choice at last.

Summarize

Summarize the story of Flora's life. Tell it to a partner or write it in a notebook. Include the following information.

1. Where did she grow up and what was her lifestyle like there?

2. Why did she leave?

3. What big choice did she have to make?

4. Where does she live now and what is her lifestyle like?

After You Read

1. The writer thinks Flora Salonik is unusual because she:
   A. went to university
   B. lives in Arusha
   C. did something unexpected
   D. speaks many languages

2. Kijungu is a town without _____ electricity.
   A. some
   B. totally
   C. the
   D. any

3. Why did Flora move to the south Maasai Steppe?
   A. to experience Dorobo life
   B. to be with her husband
   C. to be with her children
   D. to change her lifestyle

4. In paragraph 1 on page 8, who does 'they' refer to?
   A. the Dorobo people
   B. plants
   C. wild animals
   D. Flora and Loshero

5. Which of the following is NOT part of Flora's daily life in Kijungu?
   A. caring for her home
   B. gathering plants
   C. being away from her children
   D. getting milk from cattle

6. What's a suitable heading for paragraph 1 on page 11?
   A. No Contact
   B. A Family Meeting
   C. A Busy Village
   D. Contact Again

7. Which word on page 11 means 'communication'?
   A. gone
   B. contact
   C. service
   D. option

8. Why doesn't Loshero know about his wife's difficult choice?
   A. because he really doesn't like Arusha
   B. because she probably feels that she can't talk to him about it
   C. because he can't meet her family
   D. because his children didn't tell him

9. Flora feels _____ about her future.
   A. unfortunate
   B. agreeable
   C. resourceful
   D. confused

10. What view is expressed by Flora's mother?
   A. Flora should live in Arusha.
   B. Flora has a responsibility to her family.
   C. Flora has a hard life in Kijungu.
   D. Flora should call her family more often.

11. What the main purpose of page 16?
   A. to show that Flora is thinking about her life
   B. to describe Arusha
   C. to introduce Flora's past
   D. to talk about Flora's children

12. What does the writer think about Flora's final decision?
   A. It was a good decision.
   B. It was impossible to make.
   C. It was a hard choice.
   D. It was the wrong decision.

One Land — Different Lives

There are several different groups of people living in Africa. Each group has different beliefs, different methods of farming, and different ways of dressing. Three of the major groups are: the Maasai, the Bushmen, and the Yoruba.

The Maasai

The Maasai people come from Kenya and northern Tanzania. They are well known for the extremely bright colors of their clothing, and red is a favorite color for both men and women. In the past, the Maasai required only their cattle to provide them with all the food and drink they needed to survive. Even cattle blood was an important food for them at one time.

The Maasai used to constantly move their cattle around so that they would always have fresh grass to eat. Today, however, there is often not enough land for the Maasai to raise and feed large groups of cattle. As a result, some of them now have to grow crops, such as rice and vegetables. Some must also work on other people's farms.

Young Maasai Men in Traditional Red Clothing

A Bushmen Family Near Their Hut

The Bushmen

The Bushmen are one of the oldest groups in southern Africa. The group is actually made up of many different subgroups who have lived in the area for at least 20,000 years. Recently, disagreements over land have forced many Bushmen to leave the steppes of Africa. Before that however, the Bushmen were hunter-gatherers for most of their existence. During the rainy season, they moved from place to place and built huts to live in for a few days at a time. During the dry season, they stopped moving and stayed in places where there was a supply of fresh water. In traditional Bushmen society there were no chosen leaders. Instead, all decisions were made by discussing things with other members of the local group.

The Yoruba

The Yoruba are one of the largest groups in Africa, numbering about 30 million people. Most live in Nigeria, but there are also large Yoruba populations in Benin, Ghana, and Togo. Traditionally, the Yoruba were farmers. Their method of farming helped keep their lands rich and productive. Every year for three years, they would grow a different crop on a piece of land and then let the land rest for seven years. Another special feature of the Yoruba society is their belief in over 400 individual gods.

CD 2, Track 06

Word Count: 371
Time: _____

Vocabulary List

cattle (2, 3, 4, 8)
convenience (2, 7)
crop (2, 8)
figure out (11)
hunter-gatherer (8)
hut (7)
lifestyle (3, 7, 8, 19)
livelihood (2, 4)
remote (3, 7)
restless (3, 11)
reunion (15)
row (15)
safari (12)
steppe (2, 7)
transport (3, 18)